WWGD

~ What Would Grampa Do? ~

Volume 1

BRADLEY SCOTT MALONE

Pictures by Jason D. McIntosh

Copyright © 2021 by Bradley Scott Malone.
All rights reserved.

Cover, illustrations, and book design by Jason D. McIntosh.

No part of this publication may be reproduced, stored in a retrieval system, or transmitted in any form or by any means, electronic, mechanical, photocopying, recording, or otherwise, without written permission of the publisher, except as provided by U.S.A. copyright law.

This book is a work of fiction. Names, characters, places and incidents are the product of the author's imagination or are used fictitiously.

Any resemblance to actual events, locations, or persons, living or dead, is purely coincidental.

Information about the author, sales, bookings and more may be obtained by visiting www.bradleyscottmalone.com.

First printing: May 2021

ISBN:
978-1-7371908-0-6 (pb)
978-1-7371908-1-3 (hc)
978-1-7371908-2-0 (ebook)

ACKNOWLEDGMENTS

Dr. Leland M. George, PhD
You told a confused 19 year old that he was intelligent and valuable, and you kept telling him until he believed you. Now look what you've done.

Melissa Cline Malone
You are a testament to inner strength, faith and determination.
A stone that others now lean on.

The Malone Family
Thank you for holding the jump-blanket below as I leapt from window to window instead of walking down the hall like everyone else.

Mrs. Barbara Gellner Maston - Teacher
In the midst of your own hurricane, you held umbrellas to shelter us from spring showers.

Tammy & Worden Rustemeyer
Thank you for being a very safe place during a very scary time.

Sgt. Ronald E. "CatDaddy" May (In memoriam)
A friend who spent his entire paycheck replacing shirts from his own back.

DISCLAIMER

The content of this book is solely the individual opinion of the author and is for informational & entertainment purposes only and is not intended to diagnose, treat, cure, or prevent any mental condition, disease or represent any particular recommended course of action.

You understand that this book is not intended as a substitute for consultation with a licensed practitioner, therapist or counselor. Please consult with your own physician, psychologist or other licensed professional regarding the suggestions and recommendations made in this book. The use of this book implies your acceptance of this disclaimer.

The publisher and the author make no guarantees concerning the level of success you may experience by following the advice and strategies contained in this book, and you accept the risk that results will differ for each individual. The testimonials and examples provided in this book show results of the author's experience only, which may not apply to the average reader, and are not intended to represent or guarantee that you will achieve the same or similar results.

INTRODUCTION

Ideally a book would have no order to it, and the reader would have to discover his own. – Mark Twain

Well...*What Would Grampa Do?* didn't start out as a *book*. There's no prologue, over-developed dialogue, or well thought out epilogue. There was no storyboard, character or plot development brainstorming sessions, or shrewd attention to timeline and detailed setting; no overarching, thematic tropes that you have to use to sell a book now. I plan to publish works of fiction in the future, but for now I've skipped all that wonderful normalcy for—wait for it—*a list of random experiences.* Yep. My seminal published literary work is a random assortment of oddly unrelated truths. And it took almost an entire year to assemble into something even semi-coherent. Mark Twain is smiling for sure. After all, we clearly share the same affinity for plain-spoken literature and literally never combing or trimming our hair. We are a kindred spirit indeed.

This *book* was originally intended to be a handwritten list included in my estate, a substitute for all the things I might not get to share with later generations of Malones should I somehow fall victim to COVID-19. Just *something* to leave to my *children's* children besides money, pictures, or songs they can stream—a small keepsake that can be dusted off 50 years from now and travel into the still unweathered hands of family teens. There'll be a moment of curiosity as they look at duct tape on the spine and bend down to pick up the folded, yellowed pages that will surely fall out. I imagine them being folded and randomly placed back inside other pages like a flower press. I feel for these parents also trying in vain to describe what an odd and comically dysfunctional place America was in 2021, and the unusual risk Grampa took publishing this book at all back then. And I'll bet my lunch they are met with puzzled stares as they attempt to describe what a folk singer was and why anyone on earth would want one of those. I know, I wonder sometimes too, honey.

WWGD wasn't originally intended to be a faith-based book at all, it just sort of ended up that way. After assembling all the meaningful bits and pieces from the careening, clown-car-ride season of my life, there it was, staring me back at me from the pages, like a homemade jigsaw puzzle. Every bizarre moment of my life woven together by a singular, golden thread that wound like a tapestry through every bizarre moment: The kindness, generosity, and incomprehensible patience of God—it was all there.

But let's face it, everybody sort of knows what Jesus would do, right? His no-nonsense guidance for your life is pretty well documented (best-selling book ever) and understood by pretty much everyone, regardless of religious affiliation. He split time in two. We're *familiar* with it. It's for everyone.

Instead, WWGD was written specifically for young men in a very specific season of life. That exciting and frightening time when you're just getting started on your own, you're a college guy, you're entering the workplace, or just nearing the end of your high school journey. At this point in life, the world looks like a gigantic haystack, and everyone seems to already have a needle except for you.

This unique transition from juvenile to man provides the greatest opportunity to leapfrog into permanent success, or it can tip a perfectly good life into a Looney Tunes cartoon tailspin that can be near impossible to pull out of. I know about the *latter*. This period of life is the crucible all men must pass through in the decade between the ages 17 and 27. And if you don't understand certain key concepts, reality can be a remarkably unforgiving adversary during this time. And add to that, few parents or churches feel comfortable talking on a kitchen-table level about some of these dreaded 'men's issues', so you're sort of on your own. But you know what? *Grampa* might have some answers. Boy, he has seen some stuff. Go ask *him*. Then get ready to laugh while you hold his flashlight and wonder why he still calls you 'babe' and wears the same beige Dickies work pants every day, even though he retired 15 years ago.

See Grampa has no PC filter. He's seen what works and what is galactically stupid, and everything in between. And he doesn't care if he makes you or your parents uncomfortable if it means steering you away from an easily avoidable mistake. He'll just head back out to the garage anyway. Thank God for Grampa. He will help you find a way through post-truth America, *if* you want his help. Even if it's maybe not exactly what you wanted to hear at first.

To my children's *children*, this book is the love letter from Grampa. If you're reading this, chances are I'm already gone. Now go play one of my songs on your phone for Gramma. It'll make her smile. And if you read this book completely, I share my shining accomplishment in life: A secret cure for hiccups. It works *instantly*, every time. Try it, you'll see.

Volume II is underway and will be everything I want my granddaughter to know about how to navigate the workplace, children, expectations, family, and how to get and keep the upper hand when dealing with men. But for now, I'm writing to the 19-year-old *me* who *is going to be* you, or maybe is *currently* you.

A quick reader's note—I use the term 'karma' as slang instead of referencing the biblical law of reaping and sowing. I'm not an Irish, Hindu-Buddhist. I know. Shocking.

If you want to learn more about the genesis of *What Would Grampa Do?*, or about the author and his relatively bizarre odyssey, refer to the short, mini-autobiographical section titled *About the Author*. It's 15 pages or so in the very back. Exactly where it belongs.

> Because that's where Grampa would put it.

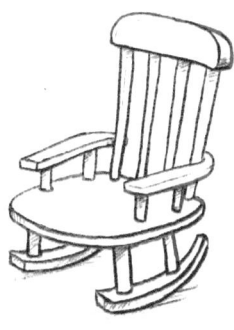

WWGD: What Would Grampa Do?
(Press # for Reality)

#1
It never pays to be a goody-2-shoes

When a normally ill-tempered person shows a moment of compassion, people often interpret it as a sign of hidden greatness or depth of character. If a person with a squeaky-clean reputation fails in any way, it's remembered forever.

#2
Practice Walking in other people's Shoes - You won't Step on their Toes as often

#3
Don't be a Brown-Noser babe, it's not worth the View

It's very tempting to laugh at all the boss's jokes and agree with their every word. Some supervisors even cultivate it for their own purposes. But it's counterproductive to your career. If you're insecure at your new job, this is an easy life-trap to fall into. Too much time in the boss's office will not only expose your entire catalog of flaws, it will give them the impression you are untrustworthy. This isn't your 10th grade art teacher that hands out A's to his pets.

#4
Being a Hero doesn't Pay well & has a lousy Dental plan

If it doesn't pertain to you, mind your own business... until you can't. Don't willingly wade into other people's business, even if they beg you. It will cost you.

#5
Honey sometimes God does send angels. If it's super important - He goes Big and sends ordinary people.

If you *ask*, God often puts the right people in your path, causes specific doors to open, and opportunities to appear that have no reasonable explanation.

#6
The Lone Ranger's mask really didn't Hide much

Don't isolate yourself, you'll get weird, but you won't realize it.

#7
If he's having lunch with your girlfriend or wife, or needs her to stay late to work, he wants to have sex with her

I don't care if it's the CEO or your best friend from grade school, there are no exceptions.

#8
Beat me, Bore me – Heck, you can even Ignore me

Young women under the age of 25 *sometimes* aren't *really* interested in nice guys until they want children. They'll deny that, but it's just too boring and predictable. They often prefer a challenge and an adventure, even if it comes with a little rejection and mistreatment. *Learn this early.*

#9
Forgiveness ain't for the Perp

Forgiveness *isn't* an act of kindness you extend *to* someone else. It's your very own get-out-of-jail-free card. Unforgiveness is a self-imposed prison. I misunderstood this. Forgiveness is about kicking hurtful people and events out of your life so **you** can live happily ever after. It's not about *them*. Most people who've hurt you wouldn't accept your forgiveness if you offered it anyway, so stop giving them free rent inside your head. Unforgiveness is setting your own La-Z-Boy on fire, then expecting someone else's fanny to get warm. Practice real forgiveness and you'll live 10 foot tall and bulletproof.

#10
Remember those who Believed in you when they are Old. You're standin' on their Shoulders.

#11
Alcohol is a liquid the pharmacy sells to Kill things. It's a lousy Prescription for filling Holes in your Heart.

But it will make brand new ones in your gut and in your wallet.

#12
If someone you Wish to love Ignores you, count your Lucky stars

It's a priceless gift to avoid wasting your time on pointless people and relationships.

#13
Don't believe everything That Pops into your head, babe

Most worrisome thoughts in your head about the future are baseless, absurdly catastrophic, negative, paranoid, exaggerated, and untrue. Well, unless the Steelers have somehow bumbled their way into the playoffs again. Otherwise, those things you're worrying about almost never come to pass in the disastrous way you imagined. Don't assign truth to thoughts just because they're bouncing around in your head. And don't make any room for ones that repeat negative things about you, *even if they are true.*

#14
Don't chase the Wrong people. You'll be too tired to notice when the Right ones walk by

2 out of every 5 people will not like you regardless of what you have in common, what you look like, or what you do for them. You won't impress 2 of the other 3.

#15
Stuff happens to Everyone. God didn't do it.

Don't blame God for the terrible things you experience and see. That will mess you up good. God *isn't* mad at you about *anything*. He also didn't cause the plane crash, the layoff, the murder, the divorce, AIDS, the cancer, the tornado, Taylor Swift, tofu burgers, or even bro country. Ok, He did do the Taylor Swift thing, but seriously, if he authorized all those terrible things, wouldn't that make God a monster bent on punishing his own creation? And you might *fear* someone like that, but you'll never *believe* they love you. Reject religious nonsense that God is trying to teach you something by sending tragedy into your life. It's not true. Read Jeremiah 29:11. Stuff happens in this very broken, fallen world...to everybody.

#16
There are things that cure Addiction. Patience isn't one of them.

Until an addict decides that their life is better sober, showering them with love and understanding is a waste of your financial resources, energy, and belongings that would be better invested elsewhere. *Unless it's your child.* Then fight like an over-caffeinated Samurai until you win them back. Otherwise, you can only replace a stolen Xbox so many times.

#17
Ken dolls make terrible Roommates

If you have to share an apartment, try to avoid moving in with a guy who is way better looking than you or has any kind of addiction. Your stuff will grow legs and your girlfriend might accidentally stop by when you aren't home.

#18
Don't just do something! Stand there!

Nope, you don't understand what they're going through. And that's A-Okay. You don't have to. Just show up when they tell you they want to be left alone, listen, and don't try to offer solutions. And bring way too much takeout.

#19
If you want the sun to Shine, sometimes you Gotta chase the Cloud away

Sometimes no matter how hard you try, some situations will just never work, especially with negative people. Sometimes you have to get rid of people or remove yourself from the situation. And if you get booted, face it, maybe *you* were the cloud.

#20
Well I'd never do something like That. Unless I could...

Don't rush to judge famous people who behave badly. They're surrounded by opportunists who tell them that gravity and karma don't apply to them. If you had millions of dollars to blow and women hurling their clothing at you, it's unlikely you'd have done much differently.

#21
There's no such thing as Casual sex

Sex is a spiritual event way, *way* more than a physical one. I know, it sounds stupid in the age of Tinder, but it's true. Part of her spirit connects with yours *forever*. That's why the first time is so incredibly magical. But *forever* is a long time, like that giant portrait tattoo on your thigh that seemed like a good idea at the time.

#22
Make sure you can Spend that $3 bill in your pocket

Make sure what you believe is actually true. Just because you believe it, doesn't make it true. Just because your dad believed it, doesn't make it *true*. Question *everything*—make people uncomfortable. The echo chamber you grew up in created the shape and color of the windows you see the world through. Go outside. If it's true, it will stand up to your questions. Some *truths* you were taught – were anything but. Proverbs 4:7

#23
Every man is his own Prophet

You will experience that which you repeatedly *speak*—good or bad. Phillipians 4:8

#24
Your call isn't really That important, there's No unusually high call volume and they're Not really helping other customers

Modern life requires us to talk to automated machines and press numbers to get what we need. It makes your anxiety level go up, but when you do finally get a human being, try asking them how their day is going, say their name back to them. Grit your teeth and be nice. *No one does that*. Even after you've waited on hold for 45 minutes and all the blood has rushed to your head. You'll be surprised how quickly your bill is corrected.

#25
never liked...who? ME?

Your friends, classmates, and coworkers go home and gripe about you, just like you do about them. They smile to your face, eat lunch with you, tell jokes, and then roll their eyes talking about you—*just like you*. You'll find out through the grapevine what they really thought of you after they are laid off, graduate or move away. Don't worry too much about what people think of you, though. Keep reading.

#26
Share your faith, however Small it appears to you. You can use words if Nothing else works

#27
Be careful with people who value Animals more than human Beings

They're likely to kick you in the ribs when you least expect it.

#28
You're standing on my Cape

Leave your parents alone after high school. They didn't get married to serve you. Carry your own weight.
They owe you *nothing*.

#29
Don't take the Easy road out, it's Haunted on the way back

If you break up with her, do it in person. You had enough courage to ask her out, now have enough to tell her it's not working out—in person. Don't do it in a text, or in a letter. And don't ghost her. She's going to get mad, cry and yell at you, and tell you she hates you in surprisingly creative ways you never imagined possible. It's going to *suck*. Do it anyway, because you get to keep your dignity. Don't be a coward.
This is one of my worst regrets.

#30
Freight trains don't take Dirt roads

You're *supposed* to have a one-track mind. You were designed to have all those desires, feelings, and motivations. If you weren't, you'd never go through all the garbage men go through to get their needs met, no one would ever get married, and there'd be no children. You get the picture.
Don't apologize for being a man.

#31
Repentance is like declaring bankruptcy, but then gettin' all new Stuff

#32
All people believe Something. Some people are really Stupid.

Be careful what you believe. If it requires blind, unquestioned obedience to a single person or organization other than Christ himself, it's a *scam*.

#33
I love you Man...

Tell your best friend you love him. It will be awkward. It will be weird. *It will also be worth it.*

#34
Wait, you **will** help me move?

Frequently invest in and reward those people who choose to value you for no apparent reason.

#35
Drinking too much Beer makes you the most Interesting Man in the World for all the wrong Reasons

#36
If she's in a string Bikini & drinking cheap Beer on a beach, your Alarm clock is about to go off

Young, beautiful, athletic people are not usually spending their free time in dark beer joints or frolicking on a beach swinging around warm bottles of flat beer. Poke fun at these ridiculous and manipulative ads. Alcohol is an *illusion* and not a prerequisite for relaxation or being an attractive adult.

#37
The More you Own, The More that Owns You

Have nice toys, buy the Camaro, the bass boat, and the 70" flat screen. Buy the Les Paul and the Harley, but don't be up to your eyeballs in debt for it. It will steal *all* the joy of owning it. Buyer's remorse is a real thing.

#38
People who own their own Islands don't care if they Ruin your day

Don't let corrupt media personalities shape your opinions.

#39
Can't sleep? God has the answer for That too.

Read the book of 1st Chronicles in the Old Testament. Nite.

#40
You will NOT always reap what You sow

At least not immediately. And *that* is the grace of God.

#41
Stop Sawin' on the branch you're a-Standin' on

Don't mistake gentleness and patience for weakness. Especially with family and supervisors. Karma happens, and often without warning.

#42
If you Feed your Body every time it asks - you will become its Short-order cook

Practice saying no to yourself occasionally when it comes to physical impulses and cravings, otherwise the wrong part of your anatomy will decide your future.

#43
If you can't afford a New vehicle... stay Out of the dealership

Never, ever assume you will successfully resist yourself.

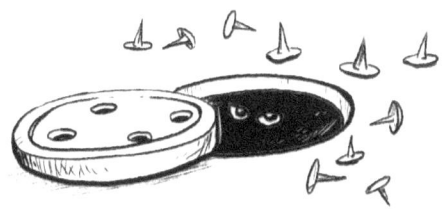

#44
It's actually OK if literally Everyone hates you

Examine yourself to see if you're being a jerk, but more importantly, don't be a people-pleaser. The only person who will never be pleased is *you*.

#45
Sometimes the Truth is the most Dishonest thing

Don't freely give your opinions of other people. If it's true, everyone probably already knows and it's likely they're OK with it. You'll look like a back-stabber by stating the obvious, and it will trigger a series of events that will shine a light on your faults instead. Nobody really likes the guy who tells it like it is. Keep it to yourself.

#46
'Honey, this bean jar is Still pretty full...'

After a woman has a baby, things *change*. After shoving a regulation NFL football out of her body because of you, you will find she is not as breathlessly excited about making another baby as when becoming pregnant seemed like the start of a Disney fairytale. And if you finally do get her in the mood, that child will be teleported to the foot of your bed or will begin fussing right on cue. Go ahead and put the bean back in the jar, Romeo.

#47
Opinions are Super useful, just like your Nipples

No one is *really* interested in your opinion unless it agrees with theirs. Well, unless you are rich or famous.

#48
Don't take the Flight of Icarus[1] honey, the return Trip is a real downer

Treat others right on the way up and a sea of hands will propel you to success with little striving on your part. Don't work 16 hours a day, abandon your family, and get 5 degrees. Those people are neck deep in debt, have massive heart-attacks in their 50s, and are on their 3rd wife. Most really great opportunities come because of your *relationships*. Doors open from people who like and trust you. Not just your qualifications. Scheme and stab people on the way up, expect a sudden karma event in your near future. Set your watch.

#49
Show me a person who takes Criticism Well and I'll show you Someone you don't want Anything from

#50
Pay close attention to her Mother and Father

It's a preview of coming attractions.

---

1 Flight Of Icarus - Traditional Greek myth & 16th century painting by Pieter Bruegel (the Elder)

#51
Santa will put your Bike together right after he takes his Beard off

Tell your child the truth early, or else they'll find a fictional version for themselves.

#52
Jesus didn't ask you to be His perfect servant

Don't get on the religious treadmill. God isn't complicated.
People are complicated.
And there's no bonus points for perfection.

#53
It's ok to be Angry and even swear a little. But then get over it.

Don't strive to be overly righteous. Religious people who pretend to be, usually aren't in secret, or are miserable on the inside attempting to be someone they're not.

#54
Hope is an actual Thing. Wishes are those little bumper sticker Fishes

A prayer that's not truly believed as having *already been answered*, is called a *wish*. Read that again slowly. And a *wish* is as useless as a homemade VHS tape of Aladdin. Go find someone who knows how to pray correctly and learn how. Mark 11:24

#55
Women want Sex as badly as You do

However, the cost of a mistake is *far* greater for her than it is for you.

#56
Just go on Over

If you suddenly feel the need to call or visit someone, just do it.
There's a reason, but you may never know it in this life.
You may arrive just in a nick of time...

#57
When you get a New car, open the trunk and put a small Scratch on the inside

Then relax and enjoy your new car.

#58
Nice guys do sometimes Finish Last

If her parents really like you and want you to get married, your relationship is probably doomed, especially if you're under 25.
It's the 'good-guy' curse and it's 100% real.
Welcome back to the Friend-Zone.

#59
A good Enemy is Easy to find

Tread lightly on another man's livelihood. Some people live one check away from being homeless.

#60
Strike 1 - Yer' out

People will only repeatedly do to you, what you repeatedly *allow* them to. If someone is kind enough to show you how they intend to mistreat you, believe them the very first time.

#61
Please hang Up and try your phone Call again

If you aren't getting anywhere with a phone customer service person, hang up and try the exact same number again. The next representative is probably not having a bad day and might not have been screamed and cursed at by the last caller.
Works almost every time.

#62
Wanna see 4 grown men Instantly turn into toddlers?

Put them in a room and tell them to play music together.

#63
Be nice until Nice is clearly Dumb

Give people a couple of chances to make things right with you. Then call an attorney and *stop talking*. Expecting people to honor a contract as they promised is sometimes unrealistic, and often expensive.

#64
Doctor, Doctor gimme the news, I got a bad Case a' Bills from you

Try to keep track of doctors who visit you in the hospital. Question every test they say is required (if you're able). You're allowed to say *no* if it makes no sense. Tell them there's no need for the EKG, the chest X-ray, and the pregnancy test every 2 hours for your back spasms. There's a reason they wait 3½ months to bill you.

#65
Being Wealthy and Rich are often Not the same. Be Wealthy.

Rich and famous people are frequently and oddly unhappy in private. Being famous is very expensive and can change overnight. The abyss of irrelevance is always nearby.

#66
After 10,000 or so hours of Practicing, you'll become an Overnight success

#67
Hurry up and Go on another Bad date

If you have a relationship that's gone bad, go on another date *as soon as possible.* Like tomorrow. Go see a movie with an old girlfriend from high school if you have to. Don't sit around stewing. Nothing makes the sun pop out again like a smiling face.

#68
If you aspire to be a Writer, be a Songwriter

People will ask you to read your stories over and over and over.

#69
Cheers fade, Cortisone fades, Chiropractors do not

Teamwork is overrated in adult life. Well, unless you're Amish or joining the Marine corps. If you're not planning on going to college on an athletic scholarship, skip high school football, wrestling, etc. altogether.
Your adult body and brain will thank you.

#70
Women are Turned On by guys with a Consuming Purpose

That's why strikingly ugly artists, actors, musicians, cops,
doctors, soldiers, preachers, and teachers
often have oddly attractive wives.

#71
Don't be in a hurry to Play God

Don't judge people based on who they fall in love with.

#72
I wonder what the UPS guy looks like in a Diaper?

You can't control every insane, random thought that pops *into* your head any more than you can decide which birds can fly *over* your head. It isn't an indication of some hidden, sinister person inside you. You can however control which ridiculous thoughts come downstairs, stay too long, eat all your pizza, plug up your toilet, borrow your keys, exit through your mouth, and change the course of your life.

#73
The Best revenge is Living Well

True, but I'd recommend skipping the revenge part altogether. Revenge is a drooling, 3-legged pit bull with fleas and a flatulence problem that eats *everything* you create.

#74
The 3 steps for Success when others Doubt You

Extend both of your index fingers.
Place the tips of those fingers directly into your ears.
Repeat steps 1 and 2.

#75
Go ahead and yell at God
if it makes you Feel better babe

If you haven't been angry with God yet, you just haven't lived long enough. He's the one who put you on this difficult planet. He understands. Psalm 139:13

#76
Drinking to relax is like exercising to be Fat

Some people can drink a little and enjoy themselves. Others can't stop until they're face down in their popcorn bowl. You won't know which one you are until you wake up on a high dive over an empty swimming pool. Avoid this risky life-trap entirely if at all possible.

#77
Be careful with Folks who Avoid eye contact when they talk to you

There's more going on in there than meets the *eye*.

#78
Good luck Dragging that Piano behind you up that Hill

Nobody can bear an emotionally wounded person for long, except other grizzled, angry people who will make you even more insufferably miserable. Learn the gift of forgiveness.

#79
Be careful where your Nose leads you, it Can't see very well and it always Hits First

Learn to sleep on it.

#80
Dude, you gotta get outta here

Try to avoid allowing yourself to get into burn-out. You'll make decisions there that you'll regret. Take every one of your vacation days each year, even if there's pressure not to. It's an entitlement, not a gift bestowed upon you by some benevolent supervisor. Get out of the office, even if you just sit home and watch Let's Make A Deal and eat an entire box of Nilla Wafers.

#81
Masturbation is a Sanity management Tool from God

Ah, the "M" word. (Shhh! We don't talk about that.) Oh stop. Newsflash—being a guy *is not easy*. Look, God delivered you with that feature from the factory for a *reason*. He intended for you to use it when you needed to. He made it possible to break the glass, grab the fire extinguisher, and put the fire out. But don't overuse this gift because it can *seriously* mess with your moods and open doors that focus your mind on things that are unwise and destructive.

#82
Treat your body Kindly and it will last a Lifetime

Practice self-care on a daily basis. Shut off that horror movie of problems that keeps rerunning inside your head. It will actually make you physically ill. Learn simple mindfulness techniques and breathing exercises. Life gets stressful, and if you don't take steps to heal yourself, no one else is going to do it for you.

#83
If it Sounds too good to be True - it's probably from the Cable company

If it comes in a presorted envelope that says "Important Documents Inside", it's a mystery call on your cell phone, has a *free* month, or shows up in your inbox, it's a gotcha-scam. You'd be surprised how easy it is to fall for them. Any company that has to resort to selling their products in these bulk methods, whatever they're selling, is likely a rip-off or totally worthless.

#84
Overtime can Cost you a ton of Money

Don't get sucked into the constant overtime trap. A lot of guys live at work and try to out-macho each other with how many hours they work. Many times, they are avoiding problems at home, or simply fleecing the company, not going the extra mile like they want to appear. You'll notice these people never seem to be able to get their work done in a 40-hour week. Don't be a passenger in that clown car. You will get burnt-out, gain weight, and be served divorce papers in front of those very same coworkers.

#85
Ignorance is bliss.
Experience is what you get after you Sign.

Realize you are feeling an adrenaline rush to get something you want. Companies know this. They put all the swindle language where they know you'll skip over it. Go find someone who understands what you're signing. Well, unless you're at a mortgage closing, then just sign everything like a drunken rock star and get the heck out of there.

#86
Say No to the 'Can' Theory of Life

Get all you can, can all you get, then sit on the can.
Reject selfish nonsense like this. Look where it's gotten us in the last 30 years. Invest in and lift up those younger than you. Leave your ladder down, mentor someone.

#87
Be kind in Secret. It feels Better.

If you are known for being generous, it will be a burden to you.

#88
Trust Jesus

Not necessarily all the people who claim to represent him.

#89
Don't forget yer' Knife - I kept it for you right Here in my Back

Some coworkers will trash you behind your back, smile at your face, then ask you about your kids in the break room. Expect it and it won't hurt...as much.

#90
Some people drink to act like Themselves

#91
Live in the Now, it's the only Place you can get Chick-fil-A

Living in the sad memories of the past or the unknown future makes you a disconnected, absent-minded zombie to the people around you.

#92
People will secretly Resent you for being Wealthy, and you will Lose friends and family relationships

Be wealthy anyway.

#93
I always figgered' you Could prob'ly do it maybe.....

The very same people who chuckled, shook their heads or rolled their eyes when you were learning, are the very first to tell you that you always had it in you. The people who saw greatness in you weren't surprised.

#94
The Tongue is the original Fiddle

Your voice contains strong vibratory energy. Positive words draw effective people to you and bring success. Negative words live on a lower frequency and magnetize low quality people and situations to you. If you wake up angry and alone,
check with your mouth.
Joshua 6:20

#95
Start humbly, end Bigly

If I'd never lived in a trailer court, I'd have no lyrics for my songs. But where you start doesn't dictate where you finish.

#96
1st impressions = 1st Promotions

First few weeks of a new job, show up a half-hour early and do not, under any circumstance, be the first to leave.
Your boss notices way more than you think he does.

#97
Just picture the Crowd in their Underwear

That boss-man jammin' on stage?
He looks super-confident, but he's *scared to death*.

#98
Where there's a Puff of smoke - there's an Inferno

If your child is acting out abnormally adult-oriented roles or behaviors, they might have seen something on TV, or they're just being a kid. Or something else *far* more destructive is happening to them—right under your nose. And they're not going to tell you. There are no *weird* kids. Put on your big-boy pants and find out what's going on.

#99
The Lack of Hope for the future is at the root of most Evil

#100
Don't judge people by their Income, big or small - Some of the Poorest people you will ever meet are Rich

#101
Be a little Rough around the edges Kiddo - Keeps folks at the proper Distance

Being super-friendly to everyone is seen as a sign of weakness. The character traits your mother tried to instill in you will get you stomped-on as a man in most circumstances outside your immediate family. People can't help it; it's just how they are.
Jesus didn't mind, but he was *Jesus*.
He could have turned them into a frog.

#102
Student loans are like Herpes

It was sort of fun at the time,
but the pain never really goes away.

#103
Find a Martha Stewart and you've found a Good thing

Find a woman who bakes and is worried about her yard.
You'll thank me later.

#104
Learn the difference between Relatives and Family and never, **ever** confuse the two

#105
Don't get Dressed up with Nowhere to go...

There isn't a 'gentleman' within a five-mile radius of a gentleman's club. Do not follow friends here, even if it's just for a bachelor party. That girl wishes she was somewhere else, and you can get yourself seriously hurt here faster than tipping over a row of Harleys.

#106
It takes 4 folk singers to change a light bulb: 1 to change it, and 3 to sing about how great the old one was

Embrace change. The past wasn't as great as you remember.

#107
Have you tried on the Emperor's New Clothes?

College can actually be a serious setback to financial success *unless* you can acquire some sort of professional licensing or certification with the degree. If lots of other people have the degree, or it's a generic liberal arts major, it will be a financial boulder you'll drag behind you for 20 years.
There's a reason it's the *only* loan you cannot default on.

#108
Being curious about someone of the same sex is 100% normal.

Oh, I can hear the haters already. Show me someone who's never had a same-sex desire, and I'll show you a *liar*. I'm not condoning or condemning anything. I'm saying this is something that unnecessarily drives people away from God for *no reason*. It doesn't *mean* anything, except that you're human. I guarantee you Christ was tempted in the exact same way, so relax.
Most importantly, don't let it keep you from God.
You're not weird, and God isn't angry with you.
Okay, maybe you're weird, but that's not the reason.
Hebrews 4:15

#109
Coworkers are sometimes like hockey Goons

At some point, that boneheaded dope will be on another team and you won't remember his name.

#110
If your church Doesn't actually Feed the poor, Find another church

#111
There's a Reason it was OK to Dump you

Figure that out first, before you look for someone new.
Unless you are into being repeatedly discarded.

#112
Don't plant your Seeds in a Wicked man's garden

Don't pay attention to evangelists who dangle God's favor in order to get you to open your wallet. God isn't out of money, and He doesn't need yours to bless you. They tend to say "sow a seed" a lot, pretend to know the future, and ride to Starbucks aboard Lear jets. They'll use your own natural desire for gain against you. And they're quite good at it. They use God as a gimmick, and it will damage your faith and your bank account at the worst possible moment. You will receive blessings when you give, but *not to these people*.

There's a special place for these counterfeits.

#113
There are reasons People don't like Christians. Don't be either one.

#1) It's easy to pretend that you're someone you're not in church. It's the original Facebook. If you think God's grace is an earned-points system, this is a real life-trap for you.

#2) Some only embrace the parts of the Bible that focus on judging others. No one ever became a lifelong follower of Christ because some sweaty guy in a polyester suit told them they were going to burn in Hell.

#114
Save the Flowers for Valentine's Day

Okay, so you had a great date and you really dig her. Wanna make sure you never see her again? Send her a bunch of roses or text/call her the following day.

#115
Your Children are Not yours

They don't *belong* to you, not even at birth. They slowly pass through you, then away from you.

#116
Leave the neighbor's Plaid sofa on the Sidewalk

Poverty thinking is a contractible disease that leads to...poverty.

#117
If you can't get Past it, try Turning around & Facing it

True guilt is God's way of nudging you to make amends.

#118
The Five Finger Rule

After the age of 30, if you can count your friends on one hand who don't let you go directly to voicemail, you are truly a *wealthy* man.

#119
Don't embarrass God

Sadly, "I'll pray for you" usually means *"Yikes"* or *"good luck with that."* Instead, say "I'm really sorry to hear about this." If you say you're going to pray for them, *do it*. Phony prayer offering is why many people think Christians and their God aren't real.

#120
Actually the apple Does roll Away from the Tree occasionally

Children are not always a reflection of their parents or their environment. Some kids just come out of the womb smoking a cigar.

#121
Don't make friends with a Rich person who tells you how Broke they are

#122
Your Name is all you will ever really Own

Unless you have a bunch of letters after your name, your reputation is all you have to offer an employer, a spouse, and your kids. Everything else can be taken away from you in lawsuits, stolen, or washed away in a flood. And remember, your children have to live with your name too.

#123
Break a child just so they Mind you, and you'll spend your 40's gluing all the Pieces back together

For the first 6 or 8 years of a child's life, they are a sponge. Their identity is being built one individual experience at a time. Childhoods are extremely hard to unlearn. Some kids you have to be very consistent and *very* strict with, or else they'll burn your house down. But remember, most kids are also desperate to obtain your approval. Childhood is baked-in after a certain point, and therapists are really expensive as an adult.

#124
Religion without a Holy Spirit experience is like owning a Diaper without the Baby

#125
Pot is like Helium

It's really funny and amusing when you first inhale, but then after a little bit you just look, feel, and sound weird.

#126
Give money to the Panhandler at the red light - Even if he does have a newer iPhone than you

Seriously. It's a great way to check yourself
and where your money truly comes from.

#127
Forgive the bully. He made you Stronger.

Besides, look at him now. See, karma *is* real.

#128
Stop being so super-Nice to people and you won't get your Feelings hurt as much

#129
You will **eventually** reap what you Daily sow

What you mentally dwell on and speak as true, you will eventually bring to pass. Good or bad. If your ship keeps running aground, have a word with the captain.

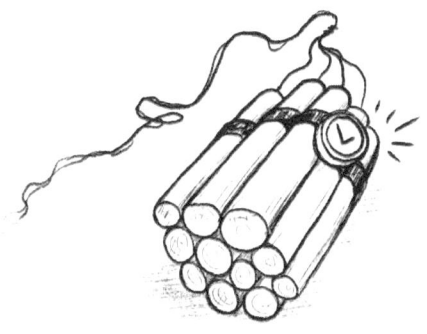

#130
Wait 2 hours before you Launch the Bomb

Emails and texts are *always*, without exception, interpreted in the most hostile manner imaginable, regardless of your most thoughtful of intentions. Whatever you type, imagine yourself screaming it at the top of your lungs, because that's exactly how it will be read. People read things into emails that aren't even there. Type that angry reply, leave it, and walk away for a while. It can wait. You probably misspelled a bunch of stuff anyway. Most of the time you'll opt to delete the nastygram entirely. Type lightly, delete often.

#131
We only Remember the very Best and very Worst of our parents

The million acts of kindness and personal sacrifice in between are never remembered. Most parents have saved their kid's life at some point. Remember - you almost walked out in front of that car.

#132
Outside of your immediate Family, people really don't Think about you as much as You think they do

Unless you have a lot of money.

#133
You don't have any Real friends that you haven't actually Screamed at

If you aren't close enough to have an angry argument, you're probably not close enough to truly be friends. They are an acquaintance and they will vanish as quickly as they appeared. Friendship that overcomes a conflict has an iron bond.

#134
If you pull the Fire alarm, expect a Fire

Never Cc or Bcc someone in an email who can negatively affect a coworker's career. Resist that temptation.
It will boomerang on you.

#135
Do not be kind to Consultants or contractors

You don't have to be a jerk, but being nice will be seen as weakness, and there's a 100% guarantee they will exploit it in some way. Unless you like being fired or getting lousy work.

#136
Jesus is a little like Elvis

If you are looking for Him above, behind, outside of you, in a book, or in a person, you'll always find that He *just left the building*.

#137
Don't Mistake your immediate coworkers for Friends

They are to be greatly valued, but in a different way. They didn't show up today to see you. And they are not your actual friends until you don't work together anymore.

#138
It's the thought that Doesn't count

Don't re-gift or give something used to someone if you can avoid doing so. It robs you of the best part of giving. A gift is an instant representation of how someone values you and vice versa.

#139
It's not his First rodeo

Don't tell the car salesman you're going to buy a car today or that you intend to pay cash. Also, be careful with all the *garbage* added on by the business office at checkout. They waste 4.5 hours of your time in the showroom in order to wear you out mentally until you'll sign *anything* just for the privilege of leaving. Wait until the very end to ask them to take the $400 pinstripes off that cost them $3. Dealerships make almost nothing off a new car sale. Those useless add-ons are the real money for them.

#140
That Jumbotron won't fit in your Living Room

If you need a dance band and a 30-foot tall LED screen to become excited enough about your faith to worship, you might find that miracles only happen once a week.

#141
Don't be Rude to salesmen

This wasn't their dream in high school.

#142
If you can both Wait until you're married to have Sex, you'll find that no one **Compares** to you

#143
Can ya gimme' a Hand pushing this thing Over the hill?

Avoid buying an American *car* that's out of warranty. Stick to full-size *trucks*—they last. Buy used Japanese cars unless you enjoy hanging out with your mechanic and paying for all the times you'll need it towed. Don't let the cheaper price fool you.

#144
Don't ever miss the Birthday party

Climbing the ladder in a small company only works for the owner's family.
And ignorant people who forget they have one.

#145
One Foot out the door
leaves You no Leg to Stand on

If you've been dumped or cheated on a couple of times, it's easy to start sabotaging relationships before someone has a chance to burn you again. You'll imagine and make up reasons to bail, because you're expecting the relationship to fail. At some point, you'll jump out of a perfectly good plane and then immediately wish you were back in it.

#146
Be careful with Super-religious people

Though friendly, their involvement in your life is purely conditional. There are legit exceptions, and you'll know them when you meet them. But for the most part, if you change churches, those very same people won't speak to you in the grocery store checkout line.

#147
Every Growing, thriving church Talks about Money

Don't get worked up over this. Ministers have to bend arms a little to get hands closer to checkbooks. If you give regularly, you'll feel closer to God and generally be more happy. Besides, somebody has to keep the heat on in the nursery. Try to do your part, but don't feel guilty for a second if you can't. Jesus was a carpenter, not an accountant.

#148
There's no Lie quite like an Extended Warranty lie

Don't buy extended warranties no matter how good the sales pitch is, or which radio personality is being compensated for peddling it. You're better off paying $1500 for a wad of gently used toilet paper instead. After you buy the car or appliance, you do not exist.

#149
If it's OK for you to Talk to your Ex, she's Seeing hers

#150
Never let her take a Vehicle to the service department Alone

She does not need headlight lubricant, different color transmission fluid, a brand new suspension, a flux capacitor, or an extra battery.

#151
Treating others with Kindness without boundaries - will Empty your Pockets and your Heart

#152
Sometimes you **Are** more important than Others

Always taking the high road with low quality people can lead to emotional exhaustion. It's just not worth it.
Tell people to #$%! off once in a while.
Some people simply don't respond to kindness.

#153
Puppy love Bites

That 12-year-old who just got their heart broken doesn't have the benefit of knowing that pain isn't permanent. Don't think it's less painful because they're young. Take them ***very seriously.***

#154
The Fastest way to make everyone Hate you is to try and make everyone Love you

There's enormous peer pressure to get along and agree with others, especially when they are criticizing someone else. If you jump in and join the trash-fest to score approval points, remember you may have to carpool with that *other* person next month.

#155
Believing you are somebody Remarkable without evidence is **stupid**

Be Stupid.

#156
If they don't sign your Paycheck or give birth to your children, their Opinion of you is utterly Meaningless

#157
Never, ever agree with Criticism of a coworker (especially if it's true)

Say something positive intentionally, even if it's "oh well, he'll get there." That two-faced coworker is saying the same about you to others.

#158
Little Horn = big Road Rage

Don't invite that kind of event into your life. Go home in one piece without a criminal record and regret. Road rage makes everyone behave in ways they wouldn't ordinarily. Sometimes people become Jekyll & Hyde when they get behind the wheel. Resist the urge. Stay off the horn, keep the single-finger salute down under the dash. Let it go intentionally.

#159
Learn the difference Between church friends, work buddies, and Personal friends

Keep them separate.

#160
Love is a technically a Four letter Word

Falling in love is easy. Getting married is even easier. She is going to wash your skid-marked underwear and you will pay credit card bills for things from Ulta and Hobby Lobby that will make your head explode. Initially, love is a mixture of physical and emotional chemistry and circumstances. If you were poor, then became rich, you have changed circumstances. And vice versa. If one of you becomes uninterested, you've changed chemistry. Have you looked at your dad recently? A woman was excited to marry him. Make sure what you have in common
is not subject to change.

#161
There are People who will work Harder for a Kind boss

The rest lean on their shovels and watch him.

#162
No one needs another Armchair reporter

Don't jump to conclusions.
You've probably never been pulled over for driving-while-black.

#163
This is gonna Hurt you more than it's Gonna hurt Me

If your little boy is angry and throwing a fit all the time, more physical discipline will probably just make him worse. I know, sounds wimpy. But you can't spank unhappiness out of a child. You do have to stand your ground, but if the depth of your relationship isn't greater than the level of your discipline, you'll create a smoldering volcano that acts out and eventually doesn't respond to anything.

#164
Money can't Buy happiness

But having a good cry in a Range Rover with hot stone massage seats and perfume atomizer is well...easier.

#165
Why God put your Eyes in the Front

If God intended for you to be always looking back, you would've been born with a rear-view mirror.

#166
If your attire in the Office is of great importance to your Employer, you probably aren't

#167
The older you get, the More you Look like yer' daddy

The older you get the more you will understand your dad and all the little things that seemed wrong with him are now wrong with you. He didn't ask for moobs and a comb-over, but he really did do the best he could. And so will you. If there were things that bothered you, then fix those with your child. Don't keep living in the past. Change the future.

#168
If it walks like a Duck...

If it seems odd that your girlfriend has so many guy 'friends' all of a sudden, it probably is. She's still playing the field. It's her right. You don't own her. Understand her girlfriends are going to run cover for her like jaded CNN anchors, and your friends will play dumb because they want to ask her out after you break up. Listen to your gut. Sometimes your gut is wrong, but not that often. Don't become a private investigator. Just walk. If you are *already* suspicious, *it ain't gonna work*.

#169
Silence can be the Loudest Sound

If the neighbor boy or girl is spending the night and your kid's room is too quiet, interrupt the silence periodically. Children have no *right* to privacy. Quiet kids are often up to no good. Besides, you don't know what's happening to that neighbor's child at home.

#170
Fair and Imbalanced

Happiness is inversely proportional to the amount of cable news consumed.

#171
Always ask Before you borrow someone else's Reputation

Always get permission before using a previous coworker or boss as a reference on a job application, never *assume* it's ok. Even if it was your best pal. Some people who smiled at you every day actually hated you.

#172
If I die, make Sure your grandmother Remarries

I wasn't that great.

#173
There are playground bullies in Khakis, too

Bite your tongue a lot at work, especially with your managers. They're under *a lot* of stress. Stuff you don't see. *However*, don't ever allow any regular coworker to bully or ridicule you personally in the workplace. Not even once. It's ok to show a little temper if that's not your normal. Don't threaten or swear, but don't put up with it. After all, they can't punch you in the stomach and take your lunch money now.

#174
Mirror, mirror on the Wall, what is wrong with Everybody?

If they're all gaslighting, ghosting you, or leaving-you-on-read, there's a reason. *You* are the common denominator.
Figure that out and the rest will sort itself out.

#175
Like a bad Neighbor

You're likely to have that random act of kindness you extended to your next door neighbor wadded up and shoved in your hat. Especially if you live in the northeast or in an urban area. Shovel your own walk, mind your own business.

#176
Always play the Two-Armed Bandit

Gamble on yourself. After all, *you* control the odds. If you are asked to take a job that you're slightly underqualified for, take it anyway. You'll figure it out or you'll get a better job because of what you learned before they fire you. Besides, it's not as easy to fire you as you think.

#177
Don't be a Scrooge

Always use a computer program to balance your bank accounts. Don't do it by hand or worse, in your head. Unless you're Ebenezer Scrooge.

#178
Tom Hanks left a message

There is no perfect house. Allow money for repairs every year.

#179
Love is an Action word

Kind words of concern and goodwill are great, but they're *meaningless* to someone in crisis. Discrete envelopes of cash in the mailbox make a great gift this holiday season. Don't worry, it comes back to you like a loaded boomerang.

#180
No one appreciates your Patience and Understanding

They appreciate you going away with the least amount of effort and with likely less than you deserve.

#181
Friendships are like Windows

They open and close. Some with little effort, others require putting your back into it. Some close, then open again years later. And some slam closed on your fingers. *Paint those shut.*

#182
If there was a Diamond on it, you're about to meet Jared

If you can still see the ring indentation on her finger, take a step back and let her sort out her life before you swing in on a vine to make everything right. Unless you want to spend the next 3 months of your life being her unpaid therapist while being constantly threatened by her ex before she goes back to him. Rebounding women will knockout foul you going to the basket. There's more fish in the sea.

#183
Well that was awkward

If you lose your temper
you will find out if people truly value you. *Quickly*.

#184
Praying is Silly

Be silly enough to believe God has *already* answered your silly prayer and He can be silly enough to bring it to pass.

#185
Live in the Mansion a little each day

Picture yourself doing the thing you dream of in your imagination. Hear what people say to you in this place. Call it done. Do it constantly. *Tell no one*. Thank me later.

#186
Honesty is all you **Don't** need

Don't share your dreams with people who will be honest with you. Honesty is *not* an ingredient in the realization of any dream.

#187
If your pot won't Boil, stop Adding ice

If something you are waiting for isn't materializing, forget about it for a while and stop dwelling on it. You may be inadvertently creating the resistance to it.

#188
And We were in our Own sight as Grasshoppers

If you're going to do something really, really big,
you're going to meet resistance *at least* equivalent to the goal.
People will tell you to go back where you came from.
That's how you'll know it's worthwhile.
Do it.
Numbers 13:33

#189
Young men use the Potential of Love to get Sex, young women use the Potential of Sex to get Love

#190
This stupid @#%#@*! printer!!*

Language a little salty? It's your spiritual check engine light. Time to go back to church and recharge your batteries.

#191
We got a Live one here!

Beware of the first coworker to invite you to lunch at your new job. He's recruiting you for his team.

#192
Opposites do Not attract - Unless you're a fridge magnet

People who are attracted to each other, *attract each other*. Opposites fight and keep divorce attorneys in business.

#193
Stop Admiring the Problem

If you're discouraged, don't tell someone all the reasons why. Unless they're a therapist or someone who can help you craft a solution, it just makes it worse.

#194
Can't have no Rainbow without a wee bit of Rain

Suffering from the onset of a bout of depression is like realizing you locked your keys in the car during a Category 4 hurricane. Hang in there. *All* storms do run out of rain eventually. Oh, and alcohol and most antidepressants are a rain dance for even more depression.

#195
For Cryin' out Loud

Force yourself to speak the things and people around you that you are grateful for. I know, it's the last thing you feel like doing. Speak it. Go on. Out loud. Especially if things are going wrong. You have to *hear* yourself say it. Try it. That is, if you don't actually *thrive* in the depression.

#196
But I like my Crocs

Be okay with people judging and disliking you.
It's happening whether you like it or not.

#197
Drive your Bus like a Boss

People you are fond of are going to get off your bus. And it's o-k. Don't plead with them to stay or ask them why. Your destination simply no longer benefits them. They're going to kick dirt on your shoes and elbow you in the gut on the way off. *It's gonna smart.* Wish them well, continue to treat them with kindness, but pull the silver handle back and close that squeaky door. Focus on the road. Others will board.

#198
No one can Stop you from realizing your Destiny

Well, except an attorney.

#199
The Voices in my Head seem to like you

The voices in your head are not your friends. They have no inherent wisdom. They're from the part of your subconscious that is tasked with trying to maintain whatever your 'normal' has come to be. That part of your mind is trained to scare you back into the familiar. It's like having Shaggy and Scooby inside your brain. Ignore those voices as much as possible. Your gut and your intention are your friends.

#200
Brain Surgery for Dummies - Chapter 1

Find out what you're good at. Do that. Everything else, find the money to pay someone who knows what they're doing.
Stay in your lane.

#201
*Tell the **Entire** truth to 3 people: Jesus, your Doctor & Your attorney*

Everyone else, keep it on a need-to-know basis. The prayers of 50 other people are no more effective than a private prayer made *correctly* by *you*. God is a God of individuals, not a scorekeeper swayed by the number of petitions.

#202
Say Cheese

Try to smile at everyone.
It's a universal way of saying I appreciate you.

#203
Imitation is the Greatest form of becoming Great

Study people who are way better at something than you are. Do everything they do. Even if you do manage to copy parts of them, there's enough of you involved that it will still be your own.

#204
Very tall fences make for Very great Neighbors

#205
Talk is Cheap and is now on Clearance

Don't pay much attention to what people tell you they care about. Watch where they spend their paycheck.

#206
A man's house is his **Woman's** castle

A house means way, way more to a woman than it does to you.

#207
Don't try to Fix her, she ain't Broken

Unless it's an appliance or her car, women often do not want a solution to their problem from you. They just want to *talk* about the problem with you. It's important.
Just listen and nod a lot.

#208
The love of Money is at the root of all Paychecks

#209
Don't make your Kids build your Casket

Make specific plans to leave your children an inheritance if you can. I know it's early to think about that, but don't be determined to bounce your last check.

#210
He's 1000 miles wide and 1/4" deep

Avoid idolizing famous people. If you were around them, you'd find they're not nearly as great as they think they are.

#211
Look for the Escalade

If you're new in town and looking for an apartment, cruise the parking lots and look at the vehicles you see. If you see really expensive full-size pickup trucks and luxury SUV's, that's where you want to live. Pay a little extra and live near people with something to lose.

#212
And Here It Is...

If you have the hiccups, take 3 **big**, extremely **exaggerated**, **super-loud** gulps of water in a row. As loud as you can make them. Do it twice if you have to. There. You're welcome. The book just paid for itself.

#213
A man who Avoids his Grandchildren is not a Bad Person

He's worse. Let someone else carry his casket.

#214
Don't listen to Drive-by critics

Don't be afraid to change jobs frequently when you are younger. Those clip-on ties who question your lack of 'loyalty' in the interview are the same empty suit, yes-man, middle-managers whose parents paid for their college and *never* promote anyone under them.

#215
So, why'd you marry Gramma anyway?

Ask your Grampa about his life. If he's honest, you will get priceless information he would never tell your dad.

#216
Don't seek Guidance from those wearing Rose-Colored glasses

That prescription is often quite blurry.

#217
The Best things in Life are hidden in Plain sight

The most rewarding things
often look like a colossal waste of your time at first.

#218
Won't you be my Fake Friend?

Social media is a counterfeit to real relationships. Don't place any real value on people you don't know personally. They wouldn't tell you your fly is down. If you haven't seen that person in over a year, and you aren't related, they do not matter.

#219
I'm sorry. That you're an Idiot

Try not to issue cigarette apologies, you know, the ones with a *but* on the end.

#220
Change their Diapers now

Look after your parents until you simply can't. Whether you feel like it or not. Your children are watching.

#221
Do as I signal, not as I do

Actors are people who are handsomely compensated for pretending to be someone they're not. Same with politicians. The loud ones are hypocrites. Disregard most everything they say. They are only relevant to other actors, news media pinheads and people who watch too much TMZ.

#222
Jesus doesn't Care who won the Football Game

#223
You got this

Cross your legs and lean back in your chair. Everyone else will calm down and relax. Then you will too.

#224
A True friend is Not honest with you

If they are truly your friend.

#225
I think you were remembering Season one

Kids are stupid, so were you.
Don't hold it against them when they're older.

#226
If you want to Reduce work stress, show up Before everyone else gets there

#227
Marry someone who Thinks you do no wrong

And you'll find you never have a reason to.

#228
Suicide is a Scam

Suicide is punting on 2nd down. It cancels your comeback by forfeiting the game. There's almost nothing you can't come back from over time. Besides, if you screw up the suicide, then you have to find another explanation for driving your dad's Buick directly off a cliff without applying the brakes.

#229
Repeat after Me

One of the most important things you can do in a job interview is say someone's name back to them while shaking hands. When they tell you their name, repeat it out loud. Now you won't forget it in 5 minutes when you need it. Write it down if you have to. Always say their name when you shake their hand on the way out, too. People like to hear their name.

#230
Shrug 'em Off

Don't invest time in people or family who shrug their shoulders
if you don't come around.
They'll call when they need something.

#231
Dad emojis rule

Send your kids text and emails out of the blue, **tell** them how
proud you are of them, and **tell** them you love them constantly
until they roll their eyes. They can't read your mind.
Then do it again.

#232
Don't watch the News,
there's Tons of money in Makin' people Mad

Unless there's an earthquake or a tornado, there's probably
nothing the outrage peddlers are saying that is of any real use to
you. As soon as they split the screen, that's your sign that there's
nothing of any further value being shared. Turn it off.
Preserve your happiness.

#233
It's not you, it's 'Me'

It's another guy. 'Me' is an odd nickname for a guy with a BMW and a trust fund...

#234
The Problems start in There somewhere

Married men want sex and to be constantly pursued physically. Married women want security and to be constantly listened to emotionally.

#235
Men fall much harder than Women and Don't get over relationships as Fast

If she just dumped a guy, you'll get to know him.

#236
*Make a **habit** of Leaning Into things that Scare the Bejeezees out of you*

#237
There's only 2 kinds of people in the world: Those who really like Jazz...and those who really do not

#238
Go with your gut: It's the Biggest thing you can see...

Make decisions relatively quickly, rely on your gut and not your logic. Your brain will talk you out of good things and lead you into safely dead ends.

#239
Gramma's Glasses had Adjustable lenses

Everybody needs a person blind enough
to see them walk on water.

#240
Don't marry your Mechanic

Don't be in a hurry to marry someone who sees all your flaws
and wants to work with you to correct them.
She will never run out of work.

#241
If she looks Too good to be True, you aren't Expecting much

#242
Abracadabra

Reality has a way of agreeing with you, especially what you *say*.
Choose your words strategically,
especially the ones you say to yourself.

#243
Why won't you ever let me talk?? Answer Me!!

Always keep your cool with an agitated woman. *Yes*, even if she hits you. At some point, even in great relationships, you're gonna have a blowout fight. It's just part of it. Know that it is her nature to push all your insecurity buttons and say things she knows will 100% make your blood boil. Your response is the difference between you and someone with a restraining order. Walk away. Let the situation de-escalate. Go home and break something of no value, like the Taylor Swift CD's she left in your truck. It's hard to accuse you of something if you aren't there. It's a no-win trap for a man to stay and fight.

#244
Well that was weird

There's a good chance your BFF growing up will never speak to you again after high school. You will never know why.

#245
Just because she Can

Women don't dress sexy because they're looking for actual sex. They just want to be better dressed than the woman on the other side of you.

#246
If you have to fight, Fight dirty

No one will remember how honorably you won,
but they will remember where the 2x4 landed.

#247
Send a woman to do a man's job...sometimes

Let your wife deal with issues at a retail store or with neighbors.
It's ok for a woman to be confrontational and agitated.
No one wants to deal with a triggered woman.
Not even another woman.

#248
Yoga pants are a thing for a Reason

Yes, they want you to notice.
However, they'd prefer you not stare.

#249
Empty tombs are Always looking for new Guests

Seldom trust a public crusader railing against social injustice. They perpetually need a villain, and at some point, it will be *you*.

#250
Cyanide Soup for the Soul

Avoid pornography at ***all costs***. It will feed you a poisonous lie that's so delicious, it's nearly impossible to unbelieve.

#251
Victimhood is a Church with no altar & no Pews, but a Million evangelists

#252
Women are often much more Attractive without makeup

But *never* say that.

#253
Does she make you laugh? She's the one.

Don't focus on super attractive women unless they knock on your door. The best loves are often the girl next door.

#254
Honest ossifer,
I'm not as thunk as you drink I is

Always leave a bar or party at, or before 11pm. Make it a rule. Nothing good ever happens after that.

#255
Don't pay the phone Thugs

Never under any circumstance pay a debt collection agency for small debts. If you're getting harassing phone calls, the company you owed money to has already sold your delinquent debt to a collection agency. Your credit is already *trashed*. Paying the collection agency does *absolutely nothing* to help you in any way.
Tell them to kiss your sassafras and hang up.
Change your phone number if you have to.
If you're in this place, every dime counts.

#256
Look, but Do Not Touch

Women are sorta like cars in a way. It's ok to check out a beautiful one, but *never* test drive one that doesn't belong to you, even if she tosses you her key and wants to put the top down for you.

#257
Pull the Cord

Most jobs are dead ends.
The last person left for a reason.
Don't complain, leave.

#258
I'll have a Budweiser and a Shot of cancer

If you absolutely must drink, do not smoke at the same time, and vice versa. Your body can only deal with so much.

#259
Looks are Everything

Don't drive junk cars *if* you can avoid it. Even if you have to save to buy an older luxury or upscale car or truck. You become what you feel like on a daily basis, and women make snap judgements based on what men drive.

#260
If you just met, and She Leaves the Club with You, she's leaving with a Complete Stranger

#261
Don't worry about what your Neighbors think of You

They don't really like you anyway.

#262
Looks fade, stomach cancer is Forever

They're called trophy wives for a reason. That's because it takes an oversized, dual-handled, 2-quart trophy cup to hold all the bourbon required to survive her.

#263
If you Find yourself in a Hole, stop Diggin'

If you piggy-back on someone else's knowledge of a subject that you know little about, you'll talk yourself into a corner and sound like an idiot. Best to stay quiet or admit you know nothing about it. Proverbs 17:28

#264
I'd like all that for Nothing & a bag of those Chips

Expecting an employer to give you more money each year outside of a cost-of-living bump is foolish and sets you up for bitterness. If you want raises, change jobs and/or get new skills frequently.

#265
Never trust Anyone who airs their own Dirty laundry in Public

Eventually, they will borrow yours.

#266
Politics are for People who don't have Enough problems

Don't be a Democrat or a Republican now. Both are religious cults with violent church picnics and their own TV channels with nothing but reruns of the *Manchurian Candidate*.

#267
Be careful Sampling another man's Rhubarb

Take your time when considering whether to become an add-a-dad. Especially if you've grown attached to her child, and being a dad makes you feel needed. She may expect you to fit into more than his old trousers.

#268
Welcome to the Family - Temp

Ignore a manager who refers to the company as a 'big family'. Corporations are giant people grinders that pay you so you can live. We're grateful for that. But a *family* it isn't.
They know this, they're just manipulating you or parroting useless company-speak.

#269
There is no Hypocrite like one with a Megaphone

Human nature is greed, lust, and power. Those who rail against those things are usually consumed with the pursuit of them.

#270
Location, Location, Desperation

Don't buy a cheap, affordable house in the wrong neighborhood because it's in your price range. You'll curse the day you bought it. The taxes will be high, and it won't increase in value no matter what you do to it. Buy a nicer home that is slightly out of your budget. You'll make it work. In a very short time, you will regret the fixer upper.

#271
If you're Gonna go, GO

Rarely, if ever, accept the counteroffer if you decide to quit. Resist the urge to leverage quitting to force an overdue raise. It's a big mistake. Remember, *you don't like it there.* You'll draw a bullseye on your back, and you will be the first person canned when the opportunity presents itself. It is the kiss of death.

#272
Can you give me a Hand with this Boot in my Mouth?

Don't get angry at your friends for revealing something you said. If you can't own it, just don't say it. You can do it.
Also cuts down on dentist bills.

#273
Sometimes you have to be 'That Dad'

If you never stand up for your child, neither will they when they get older. They will learn they are not valuable, and that it's ok for people to run over them. You don't have to excuse them, just don't join the other team. Always make sure your child sees you sticking up for them. Deal with them privately at home.
Even if you know they're guilty.

#274
At some point Mistakes become your Style

Take big risks in your career when you are young, before you have a family. Fail. Get up. Fail again. Rinse and repeat.
One day you'll wake up a rich man.

#275
Be careful what you Drink for

She's drunk and has landed in your bed. What could possibly go wrong? It doesn't matter what she *said* she wanted at 2am. It matters how she *feels* at 2pm tomorrow. Never underestimate the power of party-regret, especially in the #MeToo world.

#276
The Truth will Set you Free, But first, it will make you really, really mad

At some point you will have some glaring issue that everyone sees except for you. The needed correction will come in a manner you'd prefer it didn't.

#277
Silence is Golden

The best comeback for a snarky criticism is - *complete silence*. Literally say nothing and withdraw your eye contact. Check your phone for messages. That person will hear every possible response all at once in their head and regret opening their mouth.

#278
The Devil comes waving Scriptures and Stars

Beware of conservatives in politics who wrap themselves in the American flag or quote scripture. These are largely phony corporate shills, or empty suit front men for lobbyists and donors. They don't give a flip about you or your values.

#279
Flattery will get you an Apartment above a Beer joint while everyone else sleeps in Your house

A woman can have almost *any man* if she has access and *decides to*. We are very simple, predictable creatures. Be glad most women don't fully understand this. It's why you will see intelligent, educated men in their 50s driving rusted-out Dodge minivans, married to the eye-candy receptionist they hired 10 years ago.

#280
If you don't get it off your Chest, it will break your Heart

Grief and anger, unshared, stores up in the body and can cause all sorts of physical problems. **Talk to someone.** If it's super-personal, talk to someone in a cardigan sweater with lots of letters after their name. *Someone who can keep their mouth shut.*

#281
Biggie size my Minimum Wage

Don't freak out if your fast food order is incorrect. It's just a hamburger. Calm down. If you worked at that McJob, that side of fries wouldn't matter to you either.

#282
Will it matter a Year from Now?

Probably not. Stop worrying about it.
Call your mom, she'll worry for the both of you.

#283
We're all winners - Except for the Losers

If your kid gets a participation trophy and he lost, toss it in the garbage before you get to the van. Get him a happy meal instead, the plastic toy is way more valuable. Participation trophies are something they'll have to unlearn as an adult, and it won't be pretty.

#284
Mind if I crash here...Forever?

The next time a high school guidance counselor with 3 college degrees tells you to follow your dreams and enroll in some generic liberal arts college program, ask them if it'd be ok if you moved into their basement after graduation. And if they'd mind helping pick up the tab for the $125,000 international studies degree that qualified you to be a barista. Now *that's* a dream.

#285
Never mistreat your Mother

If you've destroyed every relationship in your life, she's the one person who will still care for you.

#286
It's easy to see the Perp walkers from a Recliner

TV cameras never come back if someone is released from custody, and *no one* is truly ever more than a few weeks away from digging through a dumpster for their breakfast. The line between barbarians and civilized people is thinner than you think.

#287
So what did you Name your new Boat again?

If it's not your company and you're not an executive, or in management, *it's just a job.* You're exchanging time for money. If you don't like that, start your own company. Seriously. Start your own LLC.

#288
No one wants to buy Wilted lettuce

The first 3 weeks you are unemployed is a crucial window of time. Most good jobs come from your network of friends, and it's easier for them to recommend you if you were just let go. You'll have plenty of time to go on vacation or binge watch *The Office* later. If you've been out 4 weeks, you're probably going to be out *at least* 4 months. After 4 weeks, people just don't want to take a chance on you as much. Don't ask me why. Even if you are perfectly qualified. This is also why you should almost *never* quit a job without another one waiting.

#289
Chapter 11 is not the Last chapter in Life

If you are confronted with a situation where you find yourself saddled with tens of thousands of $ in medical debt that you can't ever possibly repay, bankruptcy is a *good* thing. Don't get an ulcer or have a nervous breakdown over it. You will recover. Faster than you think. Remember, that hospital charged you $19 for a Tylenol and $10 for the disposable paper Dixie cup it came in. They can go $#&! in their hats.

#290
There are no Bonus points for unnecessary Honesty

When you get close and comfortable with a woman, don't be stupid and over share everything you're thinking, or worse, things that you struggle with. Over sharing to keep a conversation going will be used against you someday.

#291
Watch 'em with their Beagle

You'll know all you need to know about someone by how they treat their pets.

#292
It Ain't about You no more, Honey

If you have a baby, understand they *must* scream and fuss constantly and you'll handle it better. It's their job. They are not angry, and it's almost *never* an emergency. Take a deep breath. Put earplugs in if it helps while you change the diaper. If you leap from bed in a panic for every cranky whimper, you'll end up in the funny farm.

#293
You'll rarely meet an Old man who made Mistakes

Time has a way of softening past missteps.

#294
Work hard. Keep your nose clean. File for unemployment.

The first part of this adage might have been useful back when people retired with a gold watch and a pension after a lifetime of making other people rich. Unfortunately, the industrial revolution ended 40 years ago. *None* of that wisdom applies now. Be an effective, *indispensable* employee, *that* is your job security. You are the CEO of your life. Have a skill set that you can use to make phone calls while being escorted to your car.

#295
I have an Open-Door policy - Leave your Career by it on your way Out

Always try to resolve issues starting with your immediate supervisor, unless they have already been repeatedly asked to help. You'll only complain to the owner once.

#296
Make yourself Smile Twice a Day for no reason

Fastest way to kill the blues. Try it.

#297
If you've buried it and moved on, Put the Shovel away

Don't discuss your past with the moron who is mistake-bragging and trying to impress with their previous poor decision-making ability and calamitous life.
Give them the entire stage.

#298
Wave to the man in the Mirror

Talk to yourself in the mirror occasionally. Be nice. He's your best friend. And he has all your answers.

#299
We're all just children in Bigger clothes

Never beat the boss. Whether a game of horse, golf, or paper football in the break room, resist the temptation.
Age is mandatory, maturity is optional.

#300
Curse God and die, love – Me

Mr. Job of the Old Testament bible was a guy who went through some stuff, right? It was so bad at one point his wife told him to throw a rope over the shower curtain rod and just end it. She must've been the *wind beneath his wings*. But listen, Job 1:21 is frequently taken *way* out of context (The Lord giveth, the Lord taketh away). You'll hear well-meaning people say that all the time for just about everything. But what *Job* said wasn't intended to be a proverb, it was said out of his grief & frustration.
And by the way, *it's not true.*
Don't live by it.

#301
Don't $%&! in the bed you sleep in

Unless you are prepared to quit your job over a woman, avoid all workplace romances, even if she might be *'the one'*. Unless you are an executive, they almost always end poorly. And then it can get really awkward and complicated. You'll have to see her and her friends every day, deal with HR and all the Studly-Do-Rights who secretly had a thing for her. You are now friendless. Then if she keys your new car in the parking lot and then cries when confronted, *you* will be the one looking for a new job, not her.

#302
Ride your White Horse directly off a Cliff

Never under any circumstance get involved when a couple is spatting, no matter how much you feel like taking up for a side or putting in your 2 cents. They will get back together and *blame you for the fight.* There's a reason they're together. Butt out.

#303
Why cars come with High Beams

When it's darkest in life, you really only need to focus on what's directly in front of you and your very next turn. If you're going through hell, don't stop for a guided tour. You don't need to see the entire journey at the beginning. Just keep moving.

#304
Be the Fair-Haired child

Look after your grandmother. Don't let her be alone. Besides, how many other people on earth think you can do no wrong?

#305
Worship where there's nowhere to Park

If you have to move to a new town, find the largest church in town and attend. You'll meet the happiest people there.

#306
Can't lay your Hands off

If you aren't dead set on college, take as many vocational classes as you can. That training is free money in your pocket, even if you just build your own deck or fix your own sewer clog someday. Plus, that very same training after high school is nearly as expensive as university tuition.

#307
Avoid 'truck-mortgages'

Avoid rolling what's left of one car or truck loan into the next loan if at all possible. What's that sound? The Repo Man.

#308
Play Credit card Monopoly

If you want a high credit score (and you do) get a credit card from your credit union or bank and use it for literally every expense from coffee, to the electric bill to gasoline. Even if you have to get a prepaid card. Don't use your debit card or cash. Here's the trick—pay off the card every 2 weeks in full. Send in all the other credit card offers that start to pour in. It's computer algorithms. Wait one year and check your credit score. Boom. You're welcome. Now you can finance that car.
That usually takes many years to do.

#309
Hello my name is Kalanidhabhattabanjna, I'm here to end your career

You might have to train your H-1B replacement from Pakistan someday that can't speak much English. Have a portable skill that isn't specific to a company. And make sure you tell Zafar that we always erase the company server every two weeks, and pulling the fire alarm each morning is the way we get bagels delivered.

#310
That wasn't in the Brochure...

Avoid credit counseling. If they consolidate your credit cards into 1 *easy* payment and remove late fees, etc., your credit is still destroyed similar to declaring Chapter 11 bankruptcy. It's bankruptcy, except you still have to pay all the money back.
That's not in the radio jingle.

#311
Hey...This sucks

If it's not fun, it isn't really helping anyone,
and it's not your day job. Stop doing it.

#312
Unless your Goal is to be a Beginner, don't buy a 'beginner' musical instrument

Save your money, buy something that plays great and inspires you to pick it up. You can always sell a high-quality instrument.
Well, unless it's an accordion.

#313
Never loan your Friend or roommate Money or he shortly won't be Either one

If you give money to him, don't expect it back. If he's asking all the time, he's a leach and as soon as you stop giving him money, he'll turn on you like a tazered Rottweiler. Find better friends. He's not that cool.

#314
How's the war on Drugs going? Asking for a Friend...

Try not to be *against* anything. That which you resist, you can actually create more of. Be careful in churches that are always dancing on the devil's head. They're giving him too much airtime. Or people who are perpetually demonstrating against something. Be *for* something. One is conflict seeking, the other has a purpose.

#315
Yeah, you Heard what I said

Always let your daughter's boyfriend know you're one phone call or text away. You aren't likely to be friends, even if they get married. It's a good thing if he's a little scared of you and she doesn't like it. Sometimes even really smart gals have *shockingly* poor taste in men. Some dudes need known consequences before they will keep their act together. Same thing applies if your mom is single. Few judges will throw the book at a family member for dealing with an abuser.

#316
Pass Go, collect $200,000

Always take the free 401k matching money, even if you feel like you can't afford the contribution. After taxes, it's actually not that much difference in your actual paycheck, even if you just do 3%. Don't listen to baloney advice when you're first getting started. Keep the investments relatively conservative. You can always cash it out and eat the penalty if you are dire straits.

#317
The Difference between Men and Boys is their Choice of toys

A battery-operated baby swing may be the most important toy you'll ever buy yourself as an adult.

#318
Heroes often work for Peanuts

Cops, firemen, soldiers, and EMTs put themselves at great risk on a daily basis to serve others. If you have a chance, thank them and pick up their lunch.

#319
Shotgun marriages only work if you enjoy being Shot at

Don't be pressured into getting married solely because of an unexpected child. You'll be parents, but you'll never be married. Solving one problem isn't accomplished by creating another.

#320
Be that guy who's Always walking in Front of people

Pay for her dance lessons and buy an expensive camera. She is only a ballerina for a split second.

#321
Skinny jeans were Never really in style

Don't apologize for being a 'toxic' male. Let them criticize you. Buy the 4-wheeler, the bass boat, listen to Blake Shelton, wear the Carhartt jacket, buy your can of Skoal. They're all about a cowboy when they need a tire changed on the side of the road.

#322
It's OK to Lie once in a while. It's also called Wisdom.

If someone puts you on the spot and asks you a question that is none of their business, or by divulging what you know, you might uncover something that is damaging to someone else—it's okay to play dumb. Your integrity is more valuable than whatever they are after. A real lie is a falsehood created with the intent of manipulating others for your own gain
or to avoid accountability.

#323
Understand the human Condition - You're infected, Too

That guy who just took your parking spot isn't a bad person. The gal that ran off with the biker didn't do it to hurt you. The drunk neighbor lady who screams at her kids upstairs was abused as a child, divorced 3 times and can't get child support from any of them. The rude lady in the checkout line in front of you just had her water shut off. Life is easier if you can float at a higher elevation.

#324
Like a Frank Zappa album

There are people and things in life you will never understand.
Stop trying.

#325
Yes, women are attracted to Powerful and Wealthy men

If this bothers you, become powerful and wealthy and it won't bother you anymore.

#326
Remind her she is Still the one

Bring your wife flowers every few months for no reason. Even if she says they're a waste of money, she still wants them.

#327
Keep the merchandise Shiny

After you get married, don't turn into a slob. Wear nice shoes occasionally. Otherwise, you won't take many beans out of the jar.

#328
Stop apologizing, you're not Canadian

Apologize if you did something wrong, not if they're offended. They'll get over it.

#329
You attract more Flies with Honey than vinegar

But really, who wants flies to begin with? Be nice if that's who you are, otherwise, people see right through it.
Besides flies *love* vinegar.

#330
Fastest way from Riches to Rags is self-pity

Intentionally force yourself to stop feeling sorry for yourself after a day or so, regardless of whether it's justified. A person locked in self-pity can justify anything. Even *self-destruction*.

#331
People are our Greatest resource - Well, until they Aren't

There's a high likelihood that in the next 5 years, that publicly held company you work for, or your position in it, will be merged, off-shored, downsized, realigned, reorganized, rightsized, or acquired and liquidated by some steaming herd of invisible shareholders. Don't lose sleep over workplace drama.

#332
Chemistry - 1   You - 0

If 2 people spend enough time together, nature happens.

#333
Penny for your Thoughts?
How much for the Argument?

When a woman insists on knowing what you are thinking about, don't take the bait. Whatever you are thinking about, she will make it about her and tell you why you shouldn't be thinking it.

#334
A Clown's smile is Painted-On

Be careful with people who are super-bubbly all the time. It's not real, and neither are they.

#335
Yeah....I can't talk about that - Sorry

Never tell an employer where your next job is. Do not brag to your coworkers. Nothing to gain for you. You'll never see them again. And you might have unknowingly signed a non-compete contract when you started. After a few months they will have forgotten your name. Well, unless they need someone to blame for one of their mistakes. Then you screwed up everything the day after you left and were the worst coworker ever.

#336
Never scorch the Exit interview

If the company was going to change, it already would have. A searing critique of your boss and coworkers will follow you.

#337
Don't trash the Old Man in the Porsche

Resenting rich people will guarantee you'll never be one.

#338
Leave the Stray Kitten in the Dumpster

As a rule, women over age 21 are in their predicament because of their own choices and actions. Those aren't going to change just because you clanked along in your shining armor. Some women intentionally drown their own lifeguards. Stay off the white horse, no matter what she looks like in tight Levi's.

#339
No Good Deed shall go Unexploited

Sacrifice for others is often rewarded with even more expensive and demanding sacrifice for the exact same people.

#340
Park in between the Buick and the Peterbilt

If you're looking for a place to eat in a strange town, go where you see old folks and truckers.

#341
Good Samaritans make Lousy accountants

Count the cost of intervening, or your individual sense of right and wrong could be costly and end up helping no one.

#342
He who laughs Last - Laughs with all his Money back

If you've been ripped off on something expensive and they refuse to honor the contract, *don't panic*. Don't rant on social media, you'll lose your leverage and risk getting slapped with an expensive libel suit. Instead, go directly to your local magistrate court and file a civil complaint. It will cost a little upfront, but you'll most likely get it back. Make SURE it is served by a sheriff's deputy or constable, so it thoroughly embarrasses them. In most circumstances you'll be surprised how fast your money is returned or your work is finished out of court. Sheriff's deputies in the front yard or in the office foyer are bad optics. Judges usually take a dim view of crooks and paying employees to spend the day in court is bad for business.

#343
If talking to the Tail isn't working, try the Head

If you can't get anywhere with indifferent and rude customer service, go on LinkedIn or the company webpage. Find the CEO and send them a friendly message. Most CEO's oddly enough do read them and are keenly interested in things they can't see themselves. It's amazing how customer service sings a new tune afterward.

#344
Don't call me Sir

If people call you sir for no reason,
you're about to see they have no respect for you.

#345
Autism sucks, not having help Sucks even more

If you have a toddler who suddenly stops talking, does repeated actions for long periods of time, won't make eye contact or waves their arms wildly, go to a clinical specialist and see if they diagnose the child on the autism spectrum. If they do, get a medical disability letter. *The letter is important.* Depending on where you live, that child could then be eligible for Medicaid. Then you can get a storming mob of therapists for your child and not face financial ruin. It can make ***all*** the difference. That child may be eligible for other financial assistance like social security. *And you're gonna need it.*

#346
Don't meet too many Fat geezers

How you took care of yourself between 30-45 will determine how you live between 50-70. You're gonna gain weight, but don't allow yourself to stay obese. If you're gaining weight, stop eating after 6pm.

#347
If you're going to Burn a bridge, make sure you're not currently Standing on it

Don't become weepy and desperate just to see if you can get her back after you dumped her. You'll both lose all respect for you, even if she takes you back.

#348
That's funny weird

If it's funny, it's a joke. If it's hilarious, it's reality.

#349
Don't Kill them with Kindness, no one wants to Clean that up

#350
Yeah, we're just gonna Stay right Here, thanks

If someone takes a special interest in one of your children, it *isn't* always dangerous. But if it's a man, make sure they're never alone.

#351
Amazon can be a Jungle

Avoid buying super-expensive things from Amazon resellers or on Ebay. The actual seller is often just some sleeveless, indolent, vape-huffing scammer with a liquidation-auction pallet of returned junk in his garage. Avoid the urge to save a buck and buy from a reputable brick and mortar store.

#352
Git while the gittin's Good

Always take the job that pays more, unless it is clearly a trap-job. Even if it isn't ideal. *You'll figure it out.* Companies don't pay current employees based on what they're worth, but they do pay new employees based on current market conditions.

#353
The Squeaky wheel always gets the Grease, but if he Squeaks too Often he'll get Replaced

Pick your workplace fights carefully.

#354
Don't violate The Strangle Rule

For insurance and banking accounts, always use a company that has a physical office you can go into and get your hands around someone's throat, figuratively speaking, of course. Otherwise, your call is very important to us, please stay on the line for the next available agent.

#355
Spending other People's money is Fun

Beware of politicians who campaign on promises of 'sticking it to the man'. They intend to use that position to become rich themselves and stick it to *you*. No poor man ever signed your paycheck.

#356
Good thing yer' wife Plays that piano good

Preachers are the only people you know who must be highly educated, yet study every day until they're 75. They must be experts in their field, yet willingly live below the poverty line. They must drive a junk car and be subjected to 400 different bosses. They must be on-call 24hrs a day for free, yet selflessly visit ungrateful people who think they're overpaid. Even his 'questionable' selection of neckties is subject to endless scrutiny. He and his children are to be flawless, he must never repeat a sermon, or take a day off. He must speak painful truth but offend no one. Hug your pastor. Ministry is a thankless and often cruel calling.

#357
Be your own Private Investigator

Put a camera in your car. If there's an accident, you are 100% more likely to obtain a favorable settlement. Well, unless you drive like Grampa. People lie through their teeth when they're at fault in an accident. The camera doesn't.

#358
What doesn't kill you...well, it doesn't kill you

If you have a child with a disability or a serious medical condition, there's a high likelihood that your friends will vanish after initial sympathies. You're going to be on your own. People avoid what they don't understand. You will survive and you'll be unshakeable afterward. Expect it and it won't hurt...as much.

#359
Did you see the Video from the Christmas party? That's a shame - Everyone else has

Never drink at the office Christmas party unless you are in a senior leadership role. These are not your friends.

#360
You look Great in those, Honey

Never directly answer the "Do these make me look fat?" question.

#361
I loves Me, I loves me Not

Don't seek approval, affirmation or validation from your parents or peers. Don't place your well-being or self-esteem in the hands of others like that. They don't want that responsibility. They might not even like themselves.

#362
Check, Check, Is this thing on?

Folks who do the right thing are ordinarily humble enough not to talk about it. If they're pounding the podium about virtue, they're likely running from the absence of their own.

#363
You earn, She spends

If this bothers you, do not get married under any circumstance.

#364
Please fill out your form and submit it in the nearest Garbage can

Don't waste your time complaining to members of congress. They're there solely to represent the interests of the donors who funded their election campaign. The end.

#365
My New Year's resolution is to lose 365lbs

If you are getting married because you think you're going to have sex all the time, you're probably also optimistic about that Powerball ticket.

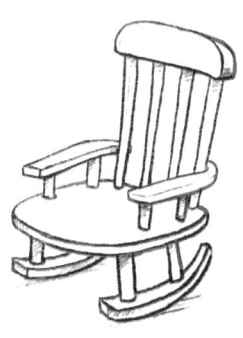

ABOUT THE AUTHOR

Matthew 10:32-33
Whosoever therefore shall confess me before men, him will I confess also before my Father which is in heaven. But whosoever shall deny me before men, him will I also deny before my Father which is in heaven.

I won't deny Him. I can't. He saved me from my greatest enemy:

Me.

1. It really was a nice Jimmy Buffett shirt...

If anything, redeemable has come from this pandemic for me, perhaps it was this: I was forced to step outside the mindless drone and din of everyday life and question it all again. What matters now? Do I even have something worthwhile to leave behind? Will I even live long enough to see my coveted first grandchild? As I began to consider my mortality with pen and paper, the exercise turned me upside down and shook literally everything from the past out of my pockets. A trickle turned into a stream, then the stream became a gushing fire hydrant like the kind that kids use to dance in during summertime heat.

As the scraps of paper piled up, one on top of the other, some scrawled on post-its, some saved on my phone apps. Suddenly those dusty, distant events from my past took on a dynamic, new energy. One event triggered the memory of another, and the exercise quickly took on a life of its own. A few weeks in, an oddly sizable list began to take shape.

Once I gathered all these snippets of my life into a pile, I struggled with how to mold them into a format that my descendants could digest and yet still find meaningful. I mean, I wouldn't want to read an autobiography written by a family member more than once, especially if I never knew them. And I can't leave them a pile of post-it notes and scribbles. That would be weird. So, the idea of a simple, informal, looseleaf notebook was discussed, then the idea of assembling them into an actual book came into being after the concept was bounced off some friends.

In the timeless words of Robert Frost, when the two roads diverged in the yellow wood, I indeed took the road less traveled by. In fact, I skipped the road less traveled entirely and hacked a needless path through the forest, all while stumbling directly beside an easily accessible freeway. But it was the path that seemed right at the time. I lacked some key understandings about life, and it sent me on unnecessary journeys down some really unfortunate roads. I could be proud and say I have no regrets, but it would be a bold-faced lie. I have a *ton* of them. But that path yielded some mighty memorable events. Some of it was nothing short of glorious. Other parts? Not so much.

So why *WWGD?* Few young men listen to their dads, right? I sure didn't. But you know, grandfathers occupy a unique position. They can speak and are often able to wade in where others can't. I never really knew either of my grandfathers. Deep down, I've always been really disappointed by that. So much history between the two of them. One was a World War II vet who flew in bombers over Europe, the other was just as colorful as people come. Or so I'm told. One grandfather was gone by the time I was 5, the other was, for whatever reason, simply uninterested. *Maybe* an engaged grandfather could've helped me with some of the hurdles I faced as a young adult. *Or* maybe I wouldn't have listened to him either.

That *'maybe'* is the inspiration for this book.

You will see numerous Christian references throughout *WWGD*. However, I don't represent any church, ministry, denomination, parachurch youth organization, nor do I claim to be any sort of bible scholar. I'm not even sure I'm qualified to suggest how many French fries to put on your salad or steak hoagie. I mean, you do have to put fries on it. Otherwise, that'd just be weird.

Those are all the things I'm not. What I *am*, is someone who's seen some...*stuff*. Maybe less than you, maybe more than you. But look, a self-help book written by some corporate ghost-author hiding behind some fake pseudonym is like getting tube socks for Christmas, right? You know, the ones with the 2 different color stripes that went up to your knees, but one always sagged. You remember, the ones you never wore to basketball practice because they made you look like a dork. But the tip from your wobbly, dazed sidekick whose eyebrows are now missing, and who's charred Jimmy Buffett concert tee is still smoking from the explosion inside his shed? Now *that's* valuable information from a friend. I believe in sharing *that* kind of information. So much so, that I put my real name on this cover.

I am also a *deeply* flawed person. I have privately shared my life as an open book with my children, with the simple hope that they wouldn't think less of me. It was more important to me that they be equipped with real-world experiences and be prepared for the *real* situations that storm and kick their way into everyday life instead of pretending that I don't suffer from the human condition. You know, like a *good* parent does.

I always hated it when people attempted to dazzle me with useless slogans or when they lobbed bible verses at me when I was going through something really difficult. They weren't really walking a mile in my shoes, rather they were inadvertently tying my shoelaces together and then asking me why I couldn't dance. They meant well, bless their pea-pickin' hearts, but I needed wisdom, not pithy axioms, or compelling, drive-by scripture quotes. Church provides larger picture wisdom, but often the minutiae of daily life can be hard to connect to scripture. And reciting condemnatory bible verses to someone who's life is already out of control is worse than saying nothing. It's like lecturing someone in a homeless encampment about diversifying their 401k, then walking away as if you've done them a favor. However, I can tell you that if you honestly share your scars with your children, your stories suddenly become wrapped in flesh, and it becomes real. The important things get across.

2. There's a Handy Cliff Right There

I wrestled with the idea of publishing this as a book for several months, and then I wrestled with it some more. Right up to the very release actually. What would people think of me? Would it be misunderstood? The inevitable questions started. Do I really need this right now? More stress in the middle of the pandemic? Is this really the time to write a book that *doesn't* ridicule men?

I was really forced to count the cost of publishing it all. It's a dangerous time to be a person of faith in America. There's no way around it. Maybe I should publish under a pseudonym, I was really unsure. The fear factor was off the charts.

In the summer of 2020, I totally chickened out and decided to put the manuscript away and leave it with my private will. I planned on making a digital video as a keepsake and leaving this document to accompany it. The end. Then the virus crisis rapidly worsened in the fall of 2020 and the brevity of my life came into much, much sharper focus. I put my hand over my eyes, and with the support and encouragement of friends, I pushed the launch button.

3. *Style is Mistakes So Fast No one Notices*

So, if I had 3 days left to live, and you were my wonderful 17- or 21-year-old grandson, what would I want to tell you? What would I want you to know before they shove that awful tube down my throat, and I bid farewell to this place? What important thing would I *forget* to tell you?

Well, first off, I'd shamelessly brag and tell you that I cured *hiccups*. That's right—*hiccups*. My crowning achievement in life? Not a nationally released album, defeating a pernicious addiction or even publishing a book. Nope. I cured hiccups using a glass of water. Take *that*, Dr. Oz.

Then I'd tell you that if you could name one of my songs or get me a Starbucks redeye I'd show you the secret. (Yes, that's in the book too). Let's get the important stuff out of the way first, right? Then I'd grab hold of your hand and I wouldn't let go of it until you promised me that you would *give Jesus a chance* if you hadn't already. After all, if He was able to sweep up all the tiny shattered bits of broken glass in my life, shake them together and breathe life back into me, *think of what He could do for you.*

I'd then promptly commence telling you how not to screw up your life. *Like I did.* As many things as I could think of. As fast as I could. I mean, how much time do we really have? As funny as I could make it. After all, I really can't be serious for very long. And the things I would mention would be short, blunt and to the point, for as long as I could keep your attention. It'd be the things I've personally experienced. The things I've had to watch others close to me experience. The *things I learned.*

My mistakes are really the only things I know for sure about in this life. All my real accomplishments could in some way be partially attributed to sheer luck, faith, and the involvement of others to one degree or another. My mistakes are what I own *entirely.* And in some ways, they're all I fully understand. Well, besides silly folk songs or my beloved Martin guitars. I can bore you to tears *yakking* about those things. I often envision a grumbling funeral director rolling his eyes, unsuccessfully attempting to close my casket lid like an overstuffed suitcase. He's having some trouble with the lid because one of my Martins is still clutched firmly in my right hand.

Anyways...

4. Dude, That's Just Way Too Much Information

"Good judgement is the result of experience and experience the result of bad judgement." -Mark Twain

In full disclosure, I have survived an uninterrupted decade of grinding alcoholism that began as simple adolescent rebellion. The inevitable Jerry Springer lifestyle that comes inside that box of Cracker Jacks was just an added bonus. I lost my eyesight for most of a day during one binge, and I have awoken in strange places with strange people and no idea how I got there.

I started as a party drinker and weekend binger in late high school. It was just what you did in the 80s as a rite of passage. You drank, you smoked cigarettes, and you had a mullet, but the weakness was there. Then off to Fairmont State University where I became a heavier, daily drinker. After a stint in the armed forces, where literally *every* problem was solved by getting wasted in the enlisted club on a nightly basis, I came back damaged goods. With a giant, angry monkey on my back who seemed to clap in my ear and pour my drinks when I played guitar, that bad monkey taught me all the secrets necessary to hide him and keep him out of sight. I walked with my hands in my pockets so no one could see my hand tremors. I became a high-functioning alcoholic.

I still deal with neurological problems on a daily basis that stem directly from that season two plus decades ago, but it's a small penalty for the abuse my body took. That monkey directed me to do all sorts of really asinine things. I have led police on high-speed chases. Twice. I stopped traffic at a busy city intersection in Georgia in 1993, exited my car and attacked another motorist in broad daylight. For simply giving me the finger. I *snapped*. Until I realized I was still in my Air Force battle dress uniform and the man's family was crying and begging me to stop from inside the car. I've been thrown through a plate glass storefront window during a bar fight and still managed to drive myself home. In the middle of the night, I swam across the Ohio river in Friendly, West Virginia pushing an inner tube full of booze, cartons of cigarettes, and a transistor radio, just to hide on an uninhabited river island.

I struggled under the weight of untreated depression, back when *real* men didn't talk about things like that. You self-medicated and moved on. That's why there were so many roadside beer joints back then. They were a type of unlicensed pharmacy for men. I survived 2 near-death experiences, one in 1988 and another in 1997. I had to deal with the untimely death of my closest friend, and a blown academic scholarship in the final semesters of my senior year. Then, a devastating workplace accident, a reconstructed arm, and the subsequent bankruptcy that followed. I lost literally everything I owned, save maybe a hat and a classical guitar with a cracked neck the pawn shop refused to take. I lived alone for an entire year with one functional hand, bleeding duodenal ulcers and a persistent smoker's cough that just never really seemed to go away. I know, it's a really lame country song. I had *issues*.

Alcohol masquerades as your very best friend as it slowly wraps itself around your identity like a python made of Rolling Rock and Crown Royal, until one day you wake up and don't know where the disease ends, and you begin. You will need it to function in public, but never really know why. You will damage yourself, nail doors of opportunity shut, and hurt others in ways that can *never* be repaired. Is that enough of a reason to grab a Pepsi?

I hope so.

After the bankruptcy, I drove a $250 car for a couple of years that took my very last dime to pay for. I have watched a man die in front of me, and I've been held at gunpoint. In the early 90s, I lived in a 1960s mobile home with cardboard-thin walls and lawn shed quality windows that moved the drapes even when they were closed. I learned the unique jeweler-like skill of knotting broken guitar strings together because I couldn't afford new ones. All this wonderfulness before the ripe old age of 27. And I came from a good, stable family.

I have been booed behind chicken wire and I've enjoyed applause from really important people. I have been surrounded by loving friends and family, and I've been so repugnant and radioactive that I couldn't buy a friend. At times, I didn't know if my life was charmed or damned. Now I know it was neither. It was what I made it.

5. Ok, we get it

So ok, I've seen some *stuff*. But so what? Everybody has. Maybe more stuff than you, maybe a lot less than you. But like my eyebrow-less friend who emerged from the burning shed, a lot of the *stuff* could have been avoided, had I been able to acquire some basic knowledge about life ahead of time. I recovered from the mistakes of my teens and 20s, but *it wasn't always clear that I would*. There were people close to me who wrote me off. And with good reason.

Some of the things I share in WWGD, if you're older, you may already know by now. You've taken your own lumps, or you steered around them because you're just a lot smarter than me. Or you had someone wise with their firm hand on your shoulder. My hat's off to you. But remember, this book wasn't really designed for you, it's the secret handbook I wished I'd had for the decade of life between the ages of 17-27. This is not a rehash of "things my dad says," or some fix-yourself-now or be-a-better-person book. There are way better writers out there for stuff like that.

So, what's the point of all this? Everybody already knows all this stuff, right? Actually, the answer is an emphatic *no*. Maybe *you* do, but you'd be shocked at the multitude of younger people who don't. Connecting the dots between actions and consequences is not as easy as it was in my generation. The only thing young people see now is what others *want* them to see. In the current, hashtag, post-truth America, young people learn by observing others in little pre-scripted, 30 second snippets on a phone screen and less and less by experiencing reality firsthand. And there is a danger there.

I was there at camp when my friend peed on the electric cattle fence out at Shiloh on the *rarely* issued TRIPLE dog-dare. I stood in awe as another friend semi-successfully paid tribute to Evel Knievel by riding an oddly impressive wheelie down the concrete steps of Zion Methodist church, only to abruptly faceplant at the bottom. I saw my best friend in the world routinely drive stumbling drunk, then one morning I woke up and he was *gone*. I didn't need an HR seminar, a life-coach or an Instagram influencer to tell me to avoid those things. The consequences of decisions can be cloaked now, and it distorts the perception of reality.

Further, the principles that worked for my dad's generation *kind of* worked for mine to a very small degree, but that is no longer the case—*in any way*. Up is down, down is up. America *changed*. Like anyone needed to be reminded of that. Ask a millennial about the bag of goods they were sold in 2007 about incurring massive debt for a college degree in business or communications.

At one time that was very *sound* advice. Now it's a punchline.

Simply *existing* as a young adult man without being cancelled, swindled, fired, threatened, scammed, infected, buried in debt, replaced, labeled, unfriended, bankrupted, exploited, ghosted, shamed, blocked, screwed, sued or tattooed requires more wisdom than at any time in history. There's just so many conflicting ideals for what an acceptable American man is supposed to be. Men have to keep their head on a greased swivel. And at a time when we text each other in the same room, sharing meaningful life experiences with those young men is more challenging than ever before. You can *ruin your life* now with just a few keystrokes on a $10 plastic keyboard or a phone screen. A single online misstep can now cost you your job, your friends, get you sued, arrested or even get you hurt. It took me a long time and a lot of hard work to screw up my life, and I didn't even need any help. Social media made it possible to invite a torch-wielding mob to your front door with a few sentences and a middle-finger emoji.

Young people are incredibly smart now though, they're wiser in many ways than I was. They're certainly more *knowledgeable* about the world than I was. At 14, they've learned more things in the YouTube/Snapchat school of life than I understood in the first 25 years of my life. Even the things I consider very sensitive men's subjects in this book are now *laughably* tame compared to the insanity 12-year-olds watch every day on TikTok or Instagram.

Young adults will quickly scan WWGD for that which applies to them, the rest will be discarded. And that's all I could ever ask for. If religious topics make you uncomfortable, just skip over them. Trust me, I get it. I thought God hated me for the longest time. And I hated Him right back. This is just the world through one man's camera lens. And I have been many different people behind that tripod. From a frail, insecure, approval-junkie adolescent, to a disillusioned and confused college dropout, I've been lots of different people.

I encourage you to share your life with your children someday as candidly as you are able to. Don't believe you have to be a picture-perfect person to raise good kids and have a meaningful place in their lives. Don't depart earth without sharing your life with someone who could benefit from the road you've traveled.

Tell your story.

www.ingramcontent.com/pod-product-compliance
Lightning Source LLC
Chambersburg PA
CBHW020910080526
44589CB00011B/521